An exclusive edition for

for all your gift books and gift stationery

This edition first published in Great Britain in 2022
by Allsorted Ltd, Watford, Herts, UK WD19 4BG

Cover design: Milestone Creative
Layout: seagulls.net
Author: Helen Vaux

ISBN: 978-1-912295-69-2

Printed in China

10 9 8 7 6 5 4 3 2 1

The
Zero Waste
Cookbook

Thrifty/Healthy/Sustainable

Contents

Introduction

It's not easy to change the world alone, but if everyone does their bit, we have the power to make a big difference. Thinking about the impact of the waste we create in our kitchen is a great starting point, and it's something we can all do towards a more sustainable future.

The ultimate goal of 'zero waste' is exactly what it says on the tin: to leave no waste behind that impacts negatively on our environment or goes into landfill. In the kitchen, this means having no waste left after cooking a meal, including ingredients and packaging. Did you know that food waste contributes to greenhouse gas emissions? As food rots in landfill, it releases methane gas – and methane is impacting climate change faster than carbon dioxide.

The good news is that we're getting better at recycling our food waste, whether that be via local recycling collections or adding it to garden compost heaps. But wouldn't it be even better if we could reuse and repurpose leftover food and the stalks and leaves that we normally discard? This book shows you how to make the most of the commonly wasted foods. Think soggy leaves, peelings, stale bread and half-used tins of chickpeas! We've tried to keep the recipes in this book as fuss-free as possible. They are by no means perfectly 'zero' – you may find you still have leftovers. However, the idea is to minimise waste as far as possible and to inspire you to be creative with your own ideas. You'll discover eye-opening new ways to reinvent meals!

Start small and you'll be amazed what you can achieve in your kitchen … and for the planet.

Note:
Recipes marked with a (v) are vegetarian-friendly.
If cheese is required, simply swap it for vegetarian cheese.

Shop smart
and plan ahead

Minimising your kitchen waste requires planning. But don't let that put you off. Remember that shopping smart will not only support sustainability and reduce your impact on the planet, it will also save your bank balance. After all, wasted food is wasted money.

Plan, plan, plan

- Creating a meal plan for the week ahead before you head to the shops not only makes life easier, it helps you use everything up. Think about how one meal might feed into the next. For example, if a recipe doesn't require a whole head of cabbage, which other recipe can you prepare to use up the cabbage?

- Be prepared for the unexpected! How often do you waste food because you ended up going out? Try to plan one meal a week that uses tinned or frozen food and cupboard staples. That way, if your plans change and you end up not eating at home, you won't be wasting fresh ingredients.

- Before you go shopping, check what's left in your fridge. How can you make use of it?

- Make a shopping list and stick to it!

Bring home as little waste as possible

- Take you own shopping bags with you. Whilst many stores offer bags made of compostable materials, it's better not to use them at all. You'll save yourself a few pennies too.

- Buy your fruit and vegetables loose. Don't buy a huge bag of potatoes if you know you're only going to use four. This saves on packaging and prevents waste. Take your own reusable bags and containers with you for loose items.

- Consider what's suitable for freezing – if you end up not being able to use something, freezing it for another time is ideal. (See page 8.)

- Discover refill shops and ditch the packaging. These are particularly brilliant for dry goods. Just take along a container and fill it up.

- And, of course, never go shopping when you're hungry! If you do, it's guaranteed you'll come home with extras you don't need and won't use.

It's a date

- Did you know that food that has passed its 'best before' date is safe to eat? The date simply shows when the quality of the product will start to change. Use your common sense and don't throw away food simply because it's gone past its 'best before' or 'sell by' date.

- The important date is the 'use by' date as this indicates the safety of the food. You can eat, cook and freeze food until, and on, the 'use by' date – but not after.

- Look out for food that has the longest 'use by' date. Or find some great bargains when food is reduced in price because it's going out of date. If you can't use it straight away, check if it can be frozen.

Make friends with your freezer

Gone are the days when freezers were all about where you keep your ready meals and ice cream. For the zero-waste cook, freezers are essential – and a fantastic way to minimise food waste. Reduce plastic waste by freezing items in reusable containers, bags or glass containers, such as jars.

- Write the date on everything you put in your freezer. Food doesn't freeze forever. Keep an eye on dates so nothing goes to waste, undoing all your good intentions.

- Regularly remind yourself what's in your freezer and you won't forget what you've stashed away.

- Divide food into portions before you freeze it so you only take out what you need.

- Fruit and vegetables with a high water content go mushy when defrosted. Plan to use them where that doesn't matter, for example in a sauce or crumble.

- If you've cooked too much, divide up portions and freeze them. You'll be thankful for it the following week when you're too tired to cook. Batch cooking is the business!

Store it well!

Store food in a way that helps it last longer. Most things don't spoil as quickly if they're kept in the fridge at between 3°C and 5°C.

Try lining the bottom of the fridge drawer with kitchen roll to absorb moisture and improve the longevity of green leafy veggies. Remember, though, that not everything wants to chill out! Potatoes and bread, for example, are better stored somewhere cool and dark. Tomatoes and cucumbers prefer room temperature.

Foods that produce ethylene when they're ripening – such as bananas, apples, avocados, tomatoes, melons, peaches and pears – should be stored separately to avoid spoiling the foods around them.

Ditch plastic and use glass jars, bowls, BPA silicone and reusable airtight containers to store food, and replace single-use cling film with sustainable beeswax food wraps.

Reuse, reinvent
and get creative!

Zero-waste cooking requires organisation. You might plan recipes that link neatly to each other to minimise waste ... but you can also have fun and let your imagination run wild! Think of it like an invention test – you've got some leftover beef, half a bag of spinach and a solitary carrot in the fridge: what can you make? Don't shy away from experimenting.

Use every last inch – Stems, leaves, seeds, peels, greens, ends, tops – all of these can be used in some way to reduce waste and make food stretch further.

Love the squishy stuff – Squishy fruit and veg might be a bit of a turn-off, but show it some love and you'll be rewarded. Blend up a delicious, healthy juice. Or mash it and freeze it. It might not look beautiful but don't throw away perfectly good food for that reason!

Pickle, preserve, ferment, infuse – Any gardener who encounters a glut of fruit and veg every year knows the power of preserving. Making a pickle doesn't need to be complicated or time-consuming – and you'll greatly extend the food's lifespan. Even jams can be knocked up relatively quickly (see page 92). Jars, spices/herbs, vinegar, salt and sugar – and something to be pickled or preserved – are all you need. Also, use fruit peel to infuse oils and vinegars.

Feed your garden – Remember, if you really can't use something, please, please, please compost it. Creating your own compost will feed all the goodness back into the earth. (But be sure to check out what you can and can't compost. Meat and bones, cooked rice and dairy products are big no-nos – so do your research.)

'We don't need a handful of people doing zero waste perfectly. We need millions of people doing it imperfectly.'

Anne Marie Bonneau

Starters and Soups

Asparagus soup
With potato and onion (v)

Ah, the woody ends of asparagus! So satisfying to snap off, but sadly they usually end up in the bin. Here's how to turn those ends into something useful and delicious – a creamy, warming asparagus soup.

Prep 10 mins / **Cook** 1 hr 20 mins / **Serves** 4

Ingredients

30–50 asparagus ends

2 garlic cloves, crushed

2 large potatoes, cut into small cubes

1 onion, chopped

2 tbsp olive oil

1 tsp lemon juice

Salt and pepper to taste

Method

1. Place the asparagus ends in a saucepan and cover with water. (The level of the water should be 2.5cm above the asparagus.) Bring to the boil, reduce the heat and simmer for 40 minutes.

2. Put the asparagus ends and liquid in a blender and blitz to a purée.

3. Strain the purée through a sieve into a bowl to separate the inedible pulp from the asparagus broth. (The pulp can be added to your compost.)

4. Heat the oil in a large saucepan and add the garlic, onion and potatoes. Cook over a medium heat for 10 minutes until starting to brown.

5. Add the broth to the saucepan and simmer for 20–30 minutes, or until the potatoes are soft enough to blend.

6. Put the broth and vegetables in a blender and purée until creamy and smooth. Stir in the lemon juice and season with salt and pepper.

7. Serve with a garnish of your choice. Try parmesan or chopped cooked bacon – or their vegetarian equivalents.

Tip
What can you do with leftover potato peelings? See the potato peel crisps recipe on page 64.

Broccoli stalk soup

With garlic and parmesan (v)

Stalks – the oft-forgotten part of broccoli! There's absolutely no reason why they should be discarded. They might not be cute and bubbly like a floret, but they taste just as good. Make the most of them with this quick and delicious soup.

Prep 10 mins / **Cook** 20 mins / **Serves** 4

Ingredients

1 small broccoli crown, broken into florets, and stalks, chopped (or just use stalks)

1 carrot, chopped

2 garlic cloves, crushed

1 tbsp olive oil

Salt and black pepper to taste

500ml vegetable stock

Handful of parmesan shavings (or vegetarian equivalent), to garnish

Tip

Broccoli stalks are just as nutritious as the florets, perhaps even slightly more so. If you're not a fan of soup, simply chop the stalks and add them to a stir-fry, as you would any other vegetable. Alternatively, save them to make a stock (see page 74) or toss them into a salad raw.

Method

1. Heat the oil in a large pan and then gently fry the garlic for 1–2 minutes, being careful not to let it burn.

2. Add the broccoli florets, stalks and carrot to the pan and pour in the stock.

3. Bring to the boil, then reduce the heat and cover. Simmer for 15–20 minutes, or until the broccoli stalks and carrot are tender. Season with salt and pepper.

4. Transfer the mixture to a blender and blend until smooth.

5. Serve hot with a dash of ground black pepper, a sprinkle of shaved parmesan and crusty bread.

Spicy fritters
With vegetable peelings and coriander (v)

This recipe is the saviour of all peelings. You can use anything – potato, carrot or parsnip peelings, even pea pods. Try whatever ap-peels! These fritters make a delicious starter, but you can also up their size for a veggie main course.

Prep 20 mins / **Cook** 15–20 mins / **Makes** 12

Ingredients

250g vegetable peelings, finely chopped

1 onion, finely chopped

½ lemon, juiced

1 tsp salt

½ tsp dried chilli flakes

1 tsp ground ginger

1 tsp ground cumin

1 tsp ground coriander

1 tsp turmeric

2 tsp curry powder

100g plain flour

Olive oil, for deep-frying

Ground black pepper and salt, to season

Handful of fresh coriander, roughly chopped

Method

1. In a large bowl, mix together the onion, peelings, chilli flakes, ginger, cumin, ground coriander, turmeric and curry powder. Season with pepper and salt.

2. Add the flour to the bowl and work all the ingredients together to make a dough. Leave to stand for 15 minutes. If the mixture is too dry, add a drop of water. Form the dough into 12 fritters, flattening them slightly.

3. Heat enough olive oil in a large, heavy-based saucepan for deep-frying. To test if the oil is hot enough, drop in a small piece of the dough – if it sizzles, the oil is ready.

4. In batches, carefully place the fritters into the hot oil and deep-fry for 5–6 minutes, or until crisp and golden, stirring whilst frying.

5. Remove the fritters from the saucepan using a slotted spoon, and drain on kitchen paper.

6. Serve warm, sprinkled with the fresh coriander and accompanied by a fruity chutney.

Tip

Fresh herbs work better in some recipes, but unless you use them up quickly and store them properly, they can easily go to waste. Dried herbs aren't the poor relation of fresh herbs, so don't shy away from them. Rule of thumb: If you substitute dried herbs for fresh, use a third of the amount. For example, 3 teaspoons of fresh oregano equals 1 teaspoon of dried.

Panzanella salad
With capers and olives (v)

Stale bread might not make great sandwiches but that doesn't mean you should wave goodbye to it. This summery salad combines bread with oil and vinegar, bringing it back to life and complementing the fresh salad beautifully. Perfect with a glass of crisp, white, Italian vino!

Prep 30 mins / **Serves** 4 (as a generous starter!)

Ingredients

1 yellow pepper

1 red pepper

6 large ripe tomatoes, roughly chopped

½ cucumber, diced

4 tbsp capers

20 black olives, pitted and halved

Handful of fresh basil leaves, roughly chopped (plus a few leaves extra to garnish)

200g stale bread (ciabatta works well but any will do), torn into chunks

For the dressing

6 tbsp olive oil

3 tbsp balsamic vinegar

Salt and black pepper, to season

Method

1. Preheat the grill to high. Grill the whole peppers until they start to blacken, turning them so that they're grilled all over. Remove from the grill and set aside for 10 minutes.

2. When the peppers have cooled slightly, peel, core and deseed them, and then chop roughly.

3. Put the chopped peppers, tomatoes, cucumber and basil in a large bowl. Mix in the capers and olives.

4. In a separate bowl, mix the olive oil with the balsamic vinegar and season well with salt and black pepper.

5. Ten minutes before serving, place the bread in a salad bowl and pour over the dressing so that the bread soaks it up. Add the tomato mixture and combine all the ingredients.

6. Serve garnished with a few basil leaves.

Tip
Another great
way to use up stale bread
is to turn it into crispbreads.
Simply spread stale slices of
bread with butter or olive oil and
put them in the oven until golden
brown. For a sweeter use of
stale bread, see the recipe
for bread pudding on
page 88.

Salmon cakes
With coriander and chilli

These spicy cakes are ideal for using up salmon (or any fish) and can be frozen to enjoy later. You can't beat home made fishcakes for flavour and crunch. Bonus point: Use stale bread for the breadcrumbs!

Prep 15 mins (plus 1 hr for chilling) / **Cook** 8 mins / **Makes** 6 cakes

Ingredients

2 garlic cloves, crushed

½ red onion, finely chopped

450g salmon fillets, skin off

300g breadcrumbs

2 tbsp mayonnaise

25g fresh coriander, finely chopped

½ tsp ground black pepper

1 tsp salt

1 tsp white wine vinegar

½ tsp chilli powder

2 eggs, beaten

3 tbsp olive oil (plus 4 tbsp for frying)

Method

1. Heat 3 tablespoons of olive oil in a frying pan over a medium heat. Add the red onion and sauté for 3–4 minutes, or until translucent. Add the garlic and sauté for 1 minute. Remove from the heat and set aside to cool.

2. Cut the salmon into small pieces. In a bowl, combine the salmon, sautéed onion and garlic, mayonnaise, pepper, salt, vinegar, fresh coriander and chilli powder. Stir in 40g of the breadcrumbs. Cover the bowl and place in the fridge for 1 hour.

3. When the mixture has chilled, form it into 6 cakes, each around 1.5cm thick.

4. Put the remaining breadcrumbs on a plate. Dip the cakes into the beaten egg and then dip into the breadcrumbs to coat each side.

5. Heat 4 tablespoons of oil in a frying pan over a medium heat. Fry the cakes for 3–4 minutes on each side until cooked through and golden.

6. Serve with salad.

Tip

These salmon cakes freeze brilliantly, making them ideal for using up salmon you're not able to enjoy before it goes past its best. You can substitute the salmon for other types of fish, as well as prawns. Try different flavourings too, especially if you have fresh herbs that need using up.

Cauliflower stalk nuggets
With ham and cheese

These nuggets use up tasty cauliflower stalks and any stale bread you have. You can also use broccoli stalks for some green pizazz. Vegetarian? Simply leave out the ham.

Prep 15–20 mins / **Cook** 20 mins / **Serves** 6 (makes 36 nuggets)

Ingredients

4 cauliflower stalks, cut into small pieces

1 tbsp olive oil

½ onion, finely diced

140g ham, cut into small pieces

50g cheddar cheese (or vegetarian equivalent), grated

125g plain flour

2 eggs, separated

1 tbsp fresh parsley, finely chopped

½ tsp salt

¼ tsp cayenne pepper

220g breadcrumbs (blitz stale bread in a blender)

Balsamic vinegar, to drizzle

Method

1. Preheat the oven to 220°C/200°C fan/ gas mark 7. Line a baking sheet with parchment paper.

2. Put the cauliflower stalks in a blender and pulse until finely chopped. Transfer to a large bowl.

3. Heat the olive oil in frying pan over a medium-high heat. Add the onion and cook for 3–4 minutes, or until softened. Add the onion to the bowl with the cauliflower.

4. Add the ham, cheese, flour, egg whites, salt, cayenne pepper and fresh parsley to the bowl, stirring well until combined.

5. Using a tablespoon, portion out the mixture and shape into nuggets.

6. Put the breadcrumbs on a plate. Dip the nuggets into the beaten egg yolk and then the breadcrumbs to coat.

7. Place the nuggets on the baking tray, drizzle with olive oil and bake for 20 minutes, turning halfway through, or until golden and crispy.

8. Serve hot accompanied by salad and a drizzle of balsamic vinegar.

Tip
Keeping a
well-stocked cupboard
of spices, herbs, cans
and pasta/rice will help you
turn today's leftovers into
tomorrow's feast. Dress up
leftovers and experiment
with flavours.

'Do your little bit of good where you are; it's those little bits of good put together that overwhelm the world.'

Archbishop Desmond Tutu

Mains

Salmon with watercress sauce

With asparagus and new potatoes

Two ingredients you're most likely to find loitering in your fridge? Crème fraiche and watercress (or, indeed, anything green you'd bought for a health kick). If your watercress is too limp for a salad, turn it into a sauce!

Prep 10 mins / **Cook** 15 mins / **Serves** 2

Ingredients

500ml whole milk

2 bay leaves

1 tsp black peppercorns

350g new potatoes

2 salmon fillets

75g watercress

2–3 tsp cream of horseradish

150ml crème fraiche

Salt and pepper

200g asparagus

Knob of butter

1 tbsp fresh parsley, chopped

Method

1. Put the milk, bay leaves and peppercorns in a pan to a simmer.

2. Add the salmon to the pan and poach gently for 10 minutes. Put the potatoes on to boil for 10–15 minutes.

3. For the sauce, blitz the watercress, horseradish and crème fraiche in a blender. Season with salt and pepper.

4. Steam the asparagus for 3 minutes.

5. Remove the salmon from the saucepan using a slotted spoon. Add some of the poaching milk to the watercress sauce to get your preferred consistency.

6. Drain the potatoes and stir in the knob of butter. Add the fresh parsley and mix to combine.

7. Serve the salmon with the potatoes and asparagus. Drizzle with the sauce.

Tip
Don't throw away the woody asparagus ends – see our recipe for asparagus soup on page 12.

Chicken and egg fried rice

With sweetcorn, pepper and peas

If you've roasted a chicken, chances are you'll have a handy amount left over. Perfect for sandwiches (or snacking on in the middle of the night by the light of the fridge), but how about using the leftover bird for something more exciting? This easy dish is perfect for a delicious and quick mid-week meal for all the family.

Prep 5 mins / **Cook** 10 mins / **Serves** 4

Ingredients

2 tbsp olive oil

300–500g leftover chicken, cut into small pieces or shredded

500g basmati rice

100g frozen peas

198g tinned sweetcorn, drained

1 red or green pepper, diced

6 spring onions, finely sliced

3 garlic cloves, crushed

4 medium eggs

2 tbsp sesame oil

2 tbsp soy sauce

Method

1. Cook the rice as per the packet instructions, drain and set aside.

2. Heat the olive oil in a frying pan or wok over a medium–high heat. Add the cooked rice, chicken, frozen peas, sweetcorn, pepper and three-quarters of the spring onions. Stir-fry for 3–4 minutes until heated through and the peas have thawed. Stir in the garlic and stir-fry for another minute.

3. Crack the eggs into a small bowl and whisk with a fork. Make a well in the middle of the mixture in the pan and pour in the eggs. Cook for 30 seconds without stirring, and then mix everything together. Continue to stir-fry for 1–2 minutes, then add the soy sauce and sesame oil and cook for 1 more minute.

4. Serve, garnished with the remaining spring onions.

Tip
Leftover rice?
Don't leave it living in
a Tupperware tub in the
fridge. Try the recipe for
rice frittata on page 66 or
pineapple fried rice on page
76. For tips on how to store
rice safely, see the tip
on page 77.

Chinese-style stir-fried lettuce

With garlic and spring onion (v)

It's rare that you ever require a whole head of lettuce for a recipe. Or that you need two little gem lettuces (so why do grocery stores only seem to sell them in packs of two?!). If you find yourself with a lot of leftover lettuce and can't face another sandwich, this recipe is the answer. Lettuce isn't only for salads!

Prep 10 mins / **Cook** 5 mins / **Serves** 2

Ingredients

Half a head of iceberg lettuce or 2 little gem lettuces

4 spring onions, cut diagonally (including the green tops)

1 tbsp vegetable oil

2 garlic cloves, finely chopped

1 tsp soy sauce

1 tsp sesame oil

1 tsp Shaoxing wine or dry sherry

2 red chillies, cut lengthways into strips

½ tsp sugar

Salt and freshly ground black pepper, to taste

Method

1. In a small bowl, mix together the soy sauce, sesame oil, Shaoxing wine (or sherry), sugar and black pepper. Set aside.

2. Tear up the lettuce leaves into large chunks.

3. Heat a large frying pan or wok until hot. Add the vegetable oil, garlic and chillies, plus half of the spring onions. Stir to combine.

4. Add the lettuce and stir-fry for 1 minute.

5. Add the sauce from the bowl and cook for a further minute. The ingredients in the pan should be coated in the sauce.

6. Season with salt (and more pepper if necessary).

7. Serve with rice and sprinkle with the remaining spring onions.

Tip
Add leftover cooked meat to a stir-fry – or, indeed, anything else in your fridge that needs using up. This recipe is a fantastic base for letting your imagination run wild (and reducing waste). Did you know that if you place a piece of kitchen towel in a bagged salad, it will absorb the moisture that causes the salad to go slimy?

Banana skin curry

With cashews and mustard seeds (v)

Chances are you've never used banana skin as an ingredient before. That you can use them might come as a surprise – but try this recipe and you'll find it's a very welcome surprise. You'll wonder why you've been throwing banana skins away for all these years!

Prep 10 mins (plus 1 hr to soak banana skin) / **Cook** 25 mins / **Serves** 2–3

Ingredients

4 banana skins

1 tbsp mustard seeds

80g cashews, chopped

1 onion, sliced

1 red chilli, seeds removed, sliced finely

2cm fresh ginger, grated

1 tbsp olive oil

½ tbsp turmeric

1 tsp red curry paste

1 tsp cumin powder

300ml water

Black pepper and salt

Method

1. Place the banana skins in a bowl of water with ¼ tablespoon of the turmeric. Leave them to soak for at least 1 hour.

2. Remove the banana skins from the water and remove the stalk and ends. Cut the skins in half widthways and then slice into thin batons.

3. Heat the olive oil in a large frying pan or wok over a medium heat. Add the mustard seeds. When the seeds start to pop, add the onions, ginger and red chilli. Cook for 3–4 minutes, stirring, and then add the curry paste, cumin powder and the remainder of the turmeric. Season with pepper and salt. Cook for a further 2 minutes.

4. Add the banana skins and the cashews and cook for 3–4 minutes, stirring constantly.

5. Pour in the water, bring to the boil and then leave to simmer for 15 minutes.

6. Serve with basmati rice.

Tip

If this recipe has won you over, why not try making a chutney with banana skins? Or use it in banana bread. Banana skins have been used as an ingredient in Asian and South American cooking for hundreds of years, so there are plenty of recipes to discover.

Savoury bread pudding
With ham and cheese

Bread pudding isn't just for the sweet-toothed (but do try the recipe on page 88!). When you've got a loaf in the cupboard that's going as hard as a rock, use it to create something savoury. The birds won't thank you, but the planet will!

Prep 20 mins / **Cook** 1 hr / **Serves** 4

Ingredients

350g bread

2 tbsp olive oil

5 shallots, chopped

10 eggs

½ tsp salt

475ml whole milk

475ml double cream

½ tsp ground black pepper (plus extra for topping)

¼ tsp ground nutmeg

115g cooked ham, sliced and cut into thin strips

1 tbsp Dijon mustard

1 handful fresh thyme, chopped

85g cheddar cheese, grated (plus 55g for topping)

Fresh parsley, chopped, to garnish

Method

1. Preheat the oven to 180°C/160°C fan/ gas mark 4. Lightly oil a baking dish (approximately 23 × 33cm).

2. Break the bread into small pieces and set aside.

3. In a frying pan, heat the oil over a medium heat. Add the shallots and sauté for 5 minutes until softened. Remove the pan from the heat.

4. In a bowl, whisk the eggs, salt, milk, cream, pepper, nutmeg and mustard. Pour the egg mixture over the bread. Add the shallots, ham, thyme and cheese. Combine well. Allow the mixture to sit for 10 minutes.

5. Transfer the contents of the bowl to the baking dish. Sprinkle 55g of cheese on top and finish with black pepper. Bake for 1 hour until is set.

6. Serve warm, garnished with parsley, accompanied by salad or baked beans.

Tip

Another great way
to use up bread is to make
breadcrumbs. Simply tear the
bread into pieces and whizz it up in
a food processor. You'll have a handy
supply of breadcrumbs for coating
meat and fish, crunchy toppings and
stuffing. Breadcrumbs can be used
from frozen, although it's best to
defrost them before use so
they don't go soggy.

Use-'em-all-up vegetable roast

With halloumi (v)

It's the end of the week and you're too tired to slave over the cooker. But there are loads of veg left in your fridge that need eating up! A one-tray roast is the perfect solution. Use up what you've got with the minimum of effort. And nothing brings out the richness in veggies quite like roasting.

Prep 15 mins / **Cook** 40 mins / **Serves** 4

Ingredients

(Use whatever is in your fridge, the below are just suggestions!)

1 aubergine, cut into wedges

2 courgettes, cubed

2 sweet potatoes, cut into chunky chip-sized wedges

1 red pepper, deseeded and chopped

1 butternut squash, peeled, seeds removed, and cubed

2 red onions, peeled and cut into wedges

1 small cauliflower, cut into small chunks

3 tbsp olive oil (plus extra for drizzling)

1 tbsp dried basil

225g halloumi (or vegetarian equivalent), cut into strips

Salt and black pepper to taste

Fresh sprigs of oregano, to garnish

Method

1. Preheat the oven to 220°C/200°C fan/gas mark 7.

2. Place all the vegetables, basil, olive oil, salt and pepper in a large mixing bowl and combine with your hands. Everything should be lightly coated with the oil.

3. Transfer to a large roasting tray and roast in the oven for 30 minutes. Remove and toss to turn the vegetables. Add the halloumi strips and roast for a further 10 minutes, or until all the vegetables are tender.

4. Serve, garnished with the oregano sprigs and a drizzle of olive oil.

Tip

To freeze vegetables, wash, top and tail, and then blanch them in boiling water for 3–4 minutes. (Delicate veggies, such as peas, require less time.) Once blanched, cool in cold water to stop the cooking process. Pat dry and then spread out on a tray to prevent them sticking together in the freezer. Once the veg is frozen, separate into bags or containers.

Goat's cheese and red onion tart

With beetroot and carrot greens (v)

If you buy your beetroot and carrots with their leaves (greens) still intact, don't discard their luscious locks! Much underrated, greens are a great replacement for herbs, such as parsley or tarragon, and spinach. They also make a tasty side dish when sautéed with garlic, pepper and olive oil.

Prep 35 mins / **Cook** 20–25 mins / **Serves** 4

Ingredients

2 tbsp olive oil

1 small red onion, finely chopped

150g beetroot and carrot greens, chopped

200g goat's cheese or vegetarian equivalent

1 garlic clove, crushed

4 tbsp double cream

1 tsp marjoram, dried

Salt and ground black pepper, to season

Balsamic vinegar, to drizzle

375g ready rolled shortcrust pastry

Method

1. Preheat the oven to 220°C/200°C fan/ gas mark 7.

2. In a large saucepan, heat the olive oil over a medium heat. Add the onion and cook for 3–4 minutes or until translucent. Add the chopped beetroot and carrot greens, and cook for another 4 minutes, or until the greens are tender. Remove from the heat and set aside.

3. In a bowl, use a fork to combine the goat's cheese, garlic, cream and marjoram until smooth. Season with salt and pepper to taste.

4. Use pastry to line a 23cm loose-bottomed tart tin or shallow dish. Spread the goat's cheese mixture over the pastry and scatter the beetroot and carrot greens on top. Bake the tart in the oven for 20–25 minutes, or until the crust is golden.

5. Serve warm or cold drizzled with balsamic vinegar.

Tip
Unfortunately, you can't use carrot tops to grow carrots. But you can use them to grow more carrot greens! Place your carrot tops in a bowl, cut-side down. Fill the bowl with water so the tops are covered halfway. Place the dish on a sunny windowsill and change the water daily. When the carrot tops sprout shoots, plant the tops in soil, but don't cover the shoots. Harvest the greens and enjoy!

Baked cod
With leek tops and fennel seeds

We're all guilty of discarding the tops of leeks. It's time to let leek tops shine, and this recipe does just that!

Prep 10 min / **Cook** 1 hr 5 mins / **Serves** 4

Ingredients

2–3 large leeks

1 tsp dried thyme

90ml olive oil

180ml dry white wine

60ml water

Ground black pepper and salt, to season

2 tsp fennel seeds

4 cod fillets, skins on

Sprig of fresh thyme, to garnish

Method

1. Preheat the oven to 190°C/170° fan/gas mark 5.

2. Remove the root end of the leeks and trim any brown tips from the opposite end. Cut off the white parts, slice thinly and set aside. Cut the green part (the leek top) in half lengthwise and rinse well. Pat dry.

3. Place the leek tops in a baking dish, sprinkle with thyme and drizzle with half the oil. Pour in the wine and water. Season. Cover with foil and bake for 45 minutes. Remove the foil and cook for 20 minutes.

4. Whilst the leek tops are cooking, toast the fennel seeds in a dry pan over a medium heat for 3–4 minutes. Remove from the heat and set aside.

5. Heat the remaining oil in the pan. Add the white leek and cook for 5 minutes until crispy. Transfer to kitchen paper, leaving the oil in the pan.

6. Season the cod fillets with pepper and salt. Return the pan to a medium heat and add the fillets, skin-side down. Cook for 4 minutes, then turn and sprinkle over the fennel seeds. Cook for 4 minutes more, or until the cod flakes.

7. Place a layer of leek tops on each plate, add the cod, leek whites and a sprig of thyme. Serve with creamy mash.

Tip
If you want to use leek tops in a stir-fry, simply steam for a couple of minutes to soften them up and then stir-fry as normal.

Macaroni salad

With celery and tomatoes (v)

This salad is not only a super simple way to use up celery, it also uses the delicious celery leaves. If you want to create more texture and different flavours, just pop in some pulses. Ignoring the mayonnaise (!), this is a healthy dish that will leave you satisfyingly full.

Prep 15 min / **Cook** 11 mins / **Serves** 4

Ingredients

225g dried macaroni

240ml mayonnaise

1 tbsp white wine vinegar

1 tbsp Dijon mustard

2 tsp sugar

½ red onion, finely chopped

100g celery, diced

25g celery leaves, finely chopped

200g tomatoes, diced and seeds removed

Salt and black pepper, to season

Method

1. Cook the macaroni in a large pan of boiling water for 9–11 minutes, or according to the packet instructions. Drain and set aside to cool.

2. In a bowl, mix together the mayonnaise, white wine vinegar, mustard and sugar to make the dressing. Season with salt and pepper.

3. Combine the dressing with the cooled macaroni.

4. Stir the celery, tomatoes, red onion and two-thirds of the celery leaves into the macaroni. Mix until evenly coated.

5. Serve, sprinkled with the remaining celery leaves.

Tip

Did you know you can use celery leaves instead of parsley? Just think of celery leaves as a herb and use them in the same way you would flat-leaf parsley.

Squashy tomato linguine
With anchovies and capers

Are your tomatoes too squashy to go in a crisp salad? Never fear, overripe tomatoes are perfect in pasta sauces. This is a wonderfully comforting and creamy pasta dish, which has a lovely tang from the anchovies and capers. Perfect when you're in need of something simple and filling after a long day.

Prep 10 min / **Cook** 20 mins / **Serves** 4

Ingredients

2 tbsp olive oil

2 red onions, chopped

250g dried linguine

2 garlic cloves, crushed

400g tomatoes, roughly chopped

4 anchovy fillets, chopped

1 tbsp capers, chopped

1 tbsp fresh parsley, roughly chopped, or 1 tsp dried parsley

200ml soured cream

Salt and black pepper, to season

Method

1. Heat the oil in a large pan over a medium heat. Add the onions and fry for 4–5 minutes until softened. Add the garlic and anchovies, and cook for 1 minute.

2. Add the linguine to the pan and pour over enough boiling water to generously cover. Bring to the boil, reduce the heat and simmer for 5 minutes.

3. Add the tomatoes. Continue to cook for 4–5 minutes until the linguine has cooked through and the tomatoes have broken down.

4. Drain the pasta mixture and return to the pan. Stir through the parsley, anchovies, capers and soured cream. Season to taste.

5. Serve with salad and warm crusty bread.

Tip

It's surprising what you can do with a tin of anchovies! If you find yourself with anchovies and capers to use up after making this dish, whip up a tapenade. Simply blitz the following in your food processor: black olives, capers, anchovies, garlic, a splash of lemon juice, and salt and pepper to taste. Delicious on bread.

Curried sweet potato and cabbage hash

With bacon and egg

Cabbage is one of those vegetables that we tend to use half of and then forget the rest. Most definitely comfort food, this hash is a filling main course and is also perfect for a weekend brunch.

Prep 15 min / **Cook** 25 mins / **Serves** 4

Ingredients

8 rashers of bacon, diced

2 large onions (red or white), roughly chopped

4 large handfuls of cabbage, chopped

4 tbsp olive oil (plus 1 tbsp for frying the eggs)

800g sweet potatoes, cut into small cubes no larger than 2.5cm square (washed but not peeled)

3 tsp curry powder

2 tsp ground cumin

1 tsp turmeric

Salt and black pepper, to taste

4 eggs

2 spring onions, finely sliced, to garnish

Method

1. Preheat the oven to 220°C/200°C fan/ gas mark 7.

2. Bring a pan of water to the boil, add the sweet potatoes, then reduce the heat and simmer for 5 minutes. Drain.

3. In a large roasting tray, add the potatoes, bacon, onions, oil, curry powder, turmeric and cumin. Season with salt and pepper. Toss together so everything is evenly coated.

4. Roast the mixture in the oven for 15 minutes. Remove from the oven, add the cabbage and combine well. Add more olive oil, if needed, then return to the oven for another 10 minutes, or until the sweet potatoes are cooked through.

5. Serve the curried hash topped with fried eggs and garnished with spring onion.

Tip

Still got leftover cabbage? Pickle it! Simply shred the cabbage and mix it with brine (120ml cider vinegar or red wine vinegar, 120ml water, 1 tablespoon sugar, 1 garlic clove, salt and pepper) in a large, clean jar with a lid. Leave for at least 2 hours then refrigerate. The pickled cabbage will keep in the fridge for 2–3 weeks. Delicious on burgers and in salads.

Beef stroganoff
With mustard and smoked paprika

Leftover meat doesn't need to end up in a sandwich. Try this quick and simple stroganoff to use up surplus roast beef. It works equally well with pork. Or leave out the meat and throw in all your mushrooms!

Prep 10 min / **Cook** 20–25 mins / **Serves** 4

Ingredients

400g leftover beef, sliced into strips

300g pasta

1 onion, sliced

150ml crème fraiche

150ml stock (beef or vegetable)

300g mushrooms, sliced

2 tbsp fresh parsley, chopped (plus garnish)

2 tsp smoked paprika

1 tbsp wholegrain mustard

1 tsp cornflour mixed with water

1 tbsp butter

2 tbsp olive oil

Salt and black pepper, to season

Method

1. Heat 1 tablespoon of oil in a pan and cook the onion on a low heat for 5 minutes, or until starting to caramelise.

2. Meanwhile, cook the pasta as per the instructions on the packet. Drain and set aside.

3. In a separate pan, melt the butter and 1 tablespoon of olive oil over a medium heat. Add the mushrooms and cook until golden brown. Remove from the heat and cover to keep warm.

4. Add the beef to the pan with the onion. Cook for 4 minutes over a medium heat until the beef is warmed through.

5. Stir in the crème fraiche, mustard, paprika and stock. Bring to the boil and then reduce to a simmer for 5 minutes, stirring. If the sauce is too runny, thicken it with the cornflour paste.

6. Add the mushrooms, pasta and parsley, and toss to evenly coat with the sauce.

7. Serve, sprinkled with chopped parsley. Season to taste.

Tip
Roast beef, if stored in an airtight container, will keep for 3–4 days in the fridge – plenty of time to use it for a mid-week meal after a Sunday roast. You can also freeze it. Mushrooms looking a bit sad? Simply peel off the outer layers, remove dry stalks and they're good to go again!

Monday pie

With Sunday leftovers

If you've never tried this, it's genius! It's the easiest way (apart from bubble and squeak) to use up a large portion of your Sunday roast leftovers. Minimum fuss, maximum impact.

Prep 20 min / **Cook** 30 mins / **Serves** 4

Ingredients

All your leftover cooked meat

All your leftover cooked vegetables

1 onion, roughly chopped

25g fresh rosemary, finely chopped

1 tbsp of olive oil

50g butter

50g plain flour

500ml stock

Salt and black pepper, to season

375g ready rolled shortcrust pastry

Method

1. Preheat the oven to 200°C/180°C fan/ gas mark 6.

2. Heat 1 tablespoon of olive oil and the butter in a saucepan. Add the onion and cook over a medium heat for 3–4 minutes. Stir in the rosemary.

3. Add the flour to the saucepan and cook for 1 minute, stirring constantly. Remove from the heat and gradually add the stock, stirring until the sauce thickens. Season with salt and pepper.

4. Add your cooked meat and vegetables to the saucepan. Remove from the heat.

5. Cut long strips of pastry to edge the rim of your pie dish. Spoon the filling into the dish.

6. Brush the pastry rim with beaten egg and place the remaining pastry on top. Gently press the edges together and trim off any excess pastry. Brush the pie lid with egg to glaze. Use a knife to make a couple of slits in the lid.

7. Bake in the oven for 30 minutes, or until the pastry has turned golden brown.

8. Serve with mashed potatoes or simply with baked beans (if the vegetable content of the pie isn't already enough for you!).

Tip

Depending on
how many leftovers
you have, you may need
to bulk the pie out with some
extra vegetables. Frozen peas
are an easy way to do this, as is
grated carrot. (Grated carrot
is fantastic for bulking out
leftover mince too.)

Cauliflower steaks

With herbs and garlic (v)

Leftover cauliflower often gets overlooked, crying out for you to make cauliflower cheese! If you want to do something a little different with your cauliflower, though, try roasting it. This is an incredibly simple but immensely satisfying dish with tons of sapore italiano.

Prep 10 min / **Cook** 35–40 mins / **Serves** 3–4

Ingredients

1 medium cauliflower (or enough to cut 4 'steaks' – see the method below)

2 tbsp olive oil (plus 1 tsp for drizzling)

1½ tsp dried Italian herb mix

8 cloves of garlic, skin on

Salt and black pepper, to season

Handful of fresh parsley roughly chopped, to garnish

1 lemon, for squeezing

Method

1. Preheat the oven to 190°C/170°C fan/gas mark 5.

2. Trim 3–4cm from opposite sides of the head of cauliflower and set aside. Cut the remaining cauliflower into 4 'steaks', each around 2.5cm thick. Imagine you're slicing a loaf of bread! Arrange the steaks in a large roasting tin.

3. In a small bowl, mix together the garlic cloves, 2 tbsp of olive oil and dried herbs. Spread the mixture over the top of the cauliflower steaks. Season with salt and black pepper.

4. Place the steaks in the oven, drizzle with olive oil and roast for 35–40 minutes, or until the cauliflower is tender and golden around the edges.

5. Garnish with a sprinkle of chopped parsley and a squeeze of lemon juice. Delicious served with couscous and drizzled with pesto (see recipe on page 68).

Tip
The leaf, stalk and florets of a cauliflower can all be eaten raw or cooked. Raw cauliflower is delicious in salads or on its own, accompanied by a dip. Need broccoli but don't have any? Cauliflower is interchangeable with broccoli in most recipes.

Beef chow mein
With a whole lotta veg

One-pot roasts and stir-fries are definite zero-waste heroes. Add whatever veggies need using up, substitute different leftover meats and experiment with herbs and sauces. There are no rules, so you can't really go wrong! This classic beef chow mein is simple to create and will make even the saddest of vegetables happy again.

Prep 15 mins / **Cook** 15 mins / **Serves** 4

Ingredients

500g roast beef, cut into strips

Any vegetables in the fridge that need using up (including stalks and leaves!), finely chopped or sliced

2 tbsp olive oil

4 noodle nests

3 tbsp soy sauce

2 tbsp oyster sauce

1 tbsp mirin

2 tbsp brown sugar

1 tbsp cornflour

2 tsp Chinese five spice

1 tbsp fresh coriander, roughly chopped, to garnish

Method

1. Cook the noodles according to the packet instructions. Drain and set aside.

2. In a small bowl or jug, gently whisk together the soy sauce, oyster sauce, mirin, brown sugar, cornflour and Chinese five spice.

3. In a large frying pan or wok, heat the oil and then add the vegetables. Stir-fry for 5 minutes, or until slightly tender.

4. Add the beef to the pan and stir-fry with the vegetables for 3–4 minutes until heated through.

5. Pour in the sauce, stir and simmer until all the ingredients are hot and the sauce is thick and sticky.

6. Add the cooked noodles and stir well to combine.

7. Serve piping hot with a sprinkle of fresh coriander.

Tip
By keeping a selection of sauces, such as soy and mirin, in your cupboard, you can turn any leftovers into something new and full of flavour. Mirin is mild and sweet; it adds extra depth to sauces and recipes, making it ideal for stir-fries.

55

Baked pasta
With everything and (almost) anything

Like a vegetable roast (page 36), this recipe will happily hoover up a multitude of ingredients from your fridge – leftovers, cooked veggies, that spare sausage and the 3 olives lurking at the bottom of a jar. Go a little wild with what you add – but obviously bear in mind that not ALL flavours work together!

Prep 20 mins / **Cook** 35–40 mins / **Serves** 4

Ingredients

450g dried pasta (works best with pasta that 'catches' the sauce, such as spirals, shells or rigatoni)

80g cheese (whatever you have), grated

Crème fraiche, if needed

Everything and anything – see the tips below!

Salt and black pepper, to season

Olive oil, to drizzle

Tip

What can you add to your pasta? The last bit of ham that won't fill a sandwich; the half tin of kidney beans you didn't need in a chilli; not-so-fresh herbs; squishy tomatoes; a lonely sausage; olives; some limp spinach; capers; bacon; or the two mushrooms that are close to death. Just have a look at what's in your fridge!

Method

1. Preheat the oven to 180°C/160°C fan/gas mark 4.

2. In a large pan, cook the pasta according to the instructions on the packet, drain and return to the pan.

3. Toss the cheese with the pasta.

4. Add all your chopped leftover ingredients and combine well. (If the mixture seems too dry, stir through a couple of tablespoons of crème fraiche.) Season with salt and pepper.

5. Transfer the pasta mixture to an ovenproof dish and drizzle with olive oil.

6. Bake in the oven for 35–40 minutes, or until bubbling.

7. Serve hot or cold with salad.

Teatime enchiladas
With spinach and feta (v)

Let's be honest, who doesn't have half a bag of spinach living in their fridge? The other half was delicious in that creamy pasta, but you don't fancy the rest in sandwiches. Enchiladas are the solution. Not only can you use up all the spinach, but you can easily add any peppers, tomatoes, sweetcorn or pulses that might otherwise be destined for the compost.

Prep 20 mins / **Cook** 20–25 mins / **Serves** 2–3

Ingredients

½ onion, chopped

2 garlic cloves, crushed

10g butter

200g spinach, roughly chopped

6 flour tortillas (25cm)

400g tin chopped tomatoes

250g mixed leftover veg or pulses

150g feta cheese (or vegetarian equivalent), cut into small cubes

Salt and ground black pepper, to season

1 tbsp olive oil

50g cheddar cheese (or vegetarian equivalent), grated

Method

1. Preheat the oven to 180°C/160°C fan/gas mark 4.

2. In a large pan, melt the butter over a medium heat, add the onion and sauté for 3–4 minutes until soft. Add the garlic and leftover veg and sauté for 1 minute more. Add the spinach and cook for 2–3 minutes. Season well with salt and black pepper.

3. Lay out the tortillas and divide the onion and veg mixture between them. On each tortilla, add 1 tablespoon of tomatoes and 25g of feta. Roll up the tortillas round the filling.

4. Grease a baking dish with olive oil and transfer the tortillas, seam-side down. Top with any leftover tomatoes and sprinkle over the grated cheddar.

5. Bake in the oven for 20–25 minutes, or until bubbling and the cheese has melted.

6. Serve accompanied by a green salad.

Tip

Spinach, rocket or other dark green leaves can be frozen from fresh and added to sauces, stir-fries and wilted. Or buy frozen in the first place – it's often cheaper than fresh but still full of goodness, and you can take as much as you need straight from the freezer.

Creamy pumpkin curry
With chickpeas (v)

Pumpkins aren't just for Halloween! However, if you do find yourself with a glut of pumpkin on 1 November, this recipe will make the most of it. Wonderfully warming, this pumpkin curry wraps you in a cuddle. And you can, of course, substitute any type of squash for the pumpkin. Don't forget to make the most of the seeds too (see page 82).

Prep 10–15 mins / **Cook** 20–25 mins / **Serves** 4

Ingredients

1 tbsp olive oil

3 tbsp yellow curry paste

2 onions, finely chopped

3 stalks lemongrass, softened with the flat side of a knife

1 tbsp mustard seeds

750g pumpkin (or squash), chopped into bitesize cubes

250ml vegetable stock

400ml can coconut milk

400g can chickpeas, drained

Juice of 1 lime

Salt and ground black pepper, to season

Handful of fresh mint leaves, to garnish

Method

1. In a large pan, heat the olive oil over a medium heat. Sauté the curry paste, onions, lemongrass and mustard seeds for 2–3 mins.

2. Add the cubed pumpkin to the pan and stir well so that it is coated in the paste. Add the stock and coconut milk. Bring to a simmer. Add the chickpeas and then gently cook for 15 mins, or until the pumpkin is tender and the chickpeas are heated through.

3. Stir the lime juice into the curry. Season well with salt and pepper.

4. Serve, garnished with the mint, accompanied by basmati rice and warm naan bread.

Tip
Curries like this
are perfect for freezing.
Simply let the curry cool, then
transfer it to an airtight container.
It will happily keep in the freezer for
a month. Don't forget that you can
also add in other spare veggies
you have – potatoes, carrots,
cauliflower and spinach
work brilliantly in
curries.

'Waste isn't waste
until we waste it.'

will.i.am

Sides, Snacks and Sauces

Potato peel crisps
With salt and rosemary (v)

There are a million and one uses for potato peelings – cleaning stainless steel, hiding grey hair (yes, really!) and as kindling – but the best is, of course, crisps! This easy recipe will leave you wondering why you ever ate shop-bought crisps.

Prep 5 mins / **Cook** 30 mins / **Serves** Depends on how many peelings you have!

Ingredients

Potato peelings (basically, whatever and however many you have left over – but make sure the potatoes were washed before you peeled them)

Rosemary, fresh or dried

Sea salt

Olive oil

Method

1. Preheat the oven to 200°C/180°C fan/ gas mark 6.

2. In a shallow roasting tin or on a baking tray, drizzle the peelings with a little olive oil and mix with the rosemary and salt. Spread the peelings out in the tin or tray, ready for baking.

3. Place in the oven and bake for 25–30 minutes until crisp and golden.

Tip

Experiment with whatever flavourings take your fancy. Try sea salt and malt vinegar or smoked paprika. This recipe is also a great way to use up fresh herbs that might be lurking in your kitchen.

Rice frittata
With parmesan and parsley (v)

Don't beat yourself up if you find yourself with leftover rice. Unless you're blessed with laser precision, it's an ingredient you're very likely to overestimate. The same applies to most things that start off dry! This frittata substitutes rice for potato and makes a lovely side dish. Alternatively, add it to your packed lunch or – if the sun's out – a picnic.

Prep 5 mins / **Cook** 10 mins / **Serves** 3–4

Ingredients

130g cooked rice

45g parmesan or vegetarian equivalent

4 tbsp olive oil

8 large eggs

1 tbsp fresh parsley leaves, finely chopped

½ tsp ground black pepper

½ tsp sea salt

handful of leftover green veg such as peas, asparagus or spinach

Method

1. In a large bowl, beat the eggs and then add the parmesan. Stir well to combine.

2. In a frying pan, heat 2 tablespoons of the olive oil over a medium heat. Add the cooked rice and veg, season, and stir for 2–3 minutes.

3. Add the egg and cheese mixture to the rice and veg in the frying pan. Stir until the eggs look lightly scrambled. Stir in the parsley. Remove from the heat and transfer to a bowl.

4. Heat the remaining 2 tablespoons of olive oil in the frying pan. Return the rice, egg and cheese mixture to the frying pan and use a spatula to form a patty. Cook for 3–4 minutes, making sure that the mixture doesn't stick to the side of the pan.

5. Carefully flip the frittata using the spatula, and cook for another 2 minutes on the other side.

6. Set the frittata aside to cool for a few minutes before serving.

Tip

Leftover rice is great for adding to any one-pot meals you're cooking. Stew, hotpot, chilli – bulk them out with some rice. Simply add it to the rest of the ingredients and let it soak up the flavours. It couldn't be easier – so, no more excuses for throwing rice away!

Carrot greens pesto
With spinach and cashews (v)

Instead of throwing them away, use your carrot greens (the leafy top of fresh carrots) to make delicious greens and cashew pesto. Great served with pasta, salad, in a sandwich or even as a simple dip for raw veggies. (See page 38 for a savoury tart recipe that uses carrot greens.)

Prep 10 mins / **Cook** 10 mins / **Serves** 4

Ingredients

40g carrot greens

40g spinach

1 garlic clove, chopped

63g roasted unsalted cashews

½ tsp salt

¼ tsp black pepper

120ml extra virgin olive oil

Method

1. Before starting, rinse the greens to remove any dirt. Discard any yellowed leaves and the tough stems – be sure to compost them!

2. Place all the dry ingredients in a food processor and pulse several times.

3. While the food processor is still running, slowly add the olive oil in a steady stream. Pulse the pesto until smooth.

4. Decant the pesto into a jar or container with a lid.

Tip

The pesto will last for about a week in the fridge. However, if you freeze it, it will keep for 6 months.

Cucumber and avocado salad

With lime, mint and feta (v)

Mint can run riot in your garden, so it's always useful to have recipes to hand that use as much of it as possible. You'll be spoilt for choice as mint combines beautifully with so many dishes. Try this refreshing salad for just one way to conquer your mint mountain!

Prep 35 mins / **Serves** 4

Ingredients

260g cucumber, chopped

Salt, for drawing water out of the chopped cucumber

2 small ripe avocados, peeled and chopped into 1.5cm pieces

1 tbsp fresh lime juice

12.5g fresh mint, finely chopped

75g feta (or vegetarian equivalent), crumbled

For the dressing

2 tbsp olive oil

1 tbsp fresh lime juice

Method

1. Put the chopped cucumber in a colander. Sprinkle with a generous pinch of salt and leave to rest for 30 minutes to draw out the water. After 30 minutes, pat the cucumber dry with kitchen towel.

2. While the cucumber is resting, make the dressing by whisking together the olive oil and lime juice.

3. Put the chopped avocado into a large salad bowl and toss with 1 tablespoon of lime juice.

4. Add the cucumber and dressing to the avocado, and stir well to combine.

5. Add the feta and mint. Again, mix well.

6. Serve immediately as a refreshing side.

Tip

Did you know
that you can freeze mint?
Simply wash, pat dry, remove
any stalks and chop the leaves
finely. Divide the mint up in an
ice-cube tray, add a little water
and then freeze until needed.
The ice-cube tray means
you only use what
you need!

Leftover cheese dressing
With garlic and herbs (v)

Perhaps not the most appetising-sounding recipe – but don't turn the page! Have you ever wondered how to make use of the rind still attached to a little piece of hard cheese that would risk your fingers if you grated it? This dressing is the answer. It won't taste 'cheesy', but the rind adds a delicious umami (savoury) flavour.

Prep 5 mins / **Infuse** 2 weeks

Ingredients

Rind from hard cheeses (such as vegetarian parmesan), left to dry overnight

1 garlic bulb, cloves peeled

Extra virgin olive oil

2 or 3 large sprigs of fresh herbs (such as thyme or oregano), left to dry overnight

Method

1. Trawl your fridge for end pieces of cheese with the rind still attached!

2. Put the rind in a clean jar or bottle with an airtight lid. Add the garlic cloves and herbs.

3. Fill the container with olive oil and shake gently.

4. Put the container in the fridge and leave for 2 weeks. After 2 weeks has passed, taste the oil to see if it has reached your ideal flavour. If it hasn't, simply put it back in the fridge for another few days. The longer, the stronger!

5. When the flavour suits your taste, strain the oil into another container. You can put the herbs back in if you'd like it to look pretty.

6. Infused oils will last for around 2 weeks. However, pay attention to the taste – if you notice the flavour starts to change, it is time to dispose of the oil.

Tip

This is also a great way to use up chillies and lemon rind. Be imaginative with flavours, but only make a small amount if you're not sure whether the combination will work. If it's horrible, don't forget that you can use olive oil to clean stainless steel! Apply sparingly and then buff with a soft cloth.

Chicken and vegetable stock
With plenty of peelings

The concept of stock is a straightforward one, but if you've never made one before, it's worth following a recipe to get it right. After that, you can tweak it depending on your taste and the leftover ingredients available. It's a fabulous way to use up the remnants of a roast dinner – and the rich flavours will boost any recipe.

Prep 10 mins / **Cook** 2 hrs 15 mins / **Makes** 1.5 litres

Ingredients

Carcass/bones from a cooked chicken

1 onion, roughly chopped

2 carrots, roughly chopped

3 cloves garlic, roughly chopped

Vegetable peelings and offcuts (avoid potato peelings – they'll make the stock cloudy)

Leftover cooked vegetables, if you have any

1 tsp dried thyme

2 bay leaves

1 tsp dried parsley

1 tbsp vinegar

5 black peppercorns

1,900ml cold water

Salt, to taste

Method

1. Put the chicken carcass, vegetable peelings, cooked vegetables (if using), thyme, parsley, bay leaves, peppercorns and vinegar into a large saucepan or stockpot. Season with salt to taste.

2. Cover with the cold water. Put a lid on the pan and bring to the boil. Remove the lid and reduce to a simmer for 2 hours.

3. Remove from the heat and allow to cool for 30 minutes. Strain to remove the bits.

4. Allow to cool completely and then place in the fridge. A layer of fat will harden on top of the stock – simply skim this off.

5. The stock will keep in the fridge for 4 days. Alternatively, freeze in handy portion sizes – the stock will keep in the freezer for 6 months.

Tip
You might not have enough vegetable peelings or leftover veggies from just one meal to make this stock. Keep a bag in the freezer and simply top this up with any peelings and leftovers through the week. You'll quickly build up a stash to create this delicious stock.

Pineapple fried rice
With red chilli (v)

You can never have too many recipes for leftover cooked rice! It makes a great base for creating a tasty dish with whatever you have to hand. This sweet and spicy pineapple rice can be a main dish with a few prawns or some leftover chicken thrown in, but we prefer it as an accompaniment – it's much more exciting than plain rice.

Prep 10 mins / **Cook** 15–20 mins / **Serves** 4

Ingredients

1 onion, chopped

2 carrots, peeled and grated

1 red chilli, deseeded and finely sliced

130g frozen peas, thawed

525g rice, cooked

2 garlic cloves, crushed

400g fresh pineapple, diced

2 spring onions, finely sliced

3 tbsp soy sauce

1 tsp ground ginger

1 tsp ground black pepper

2 tbsp olive oil

1 tbsp sesame oil

Method

1. In a small bowl, mix together the sesame oil, black pepper, soy sauce and ground ginger.

2. In a large frying pan, heat the olive oil over a medium heat. Add the onion and sauté for 3–4 minutes until it starts to soften and turn translucent. Add the chilli and garlic, and cook for a further minute.

3. Add the carrots and peas to the pan, and cook until the vegetables are tender, stirring continuously.

4. Stir in the rice, pineapple, spring onions and the soy sauce mixture from the small bowl. Continue cooking for 4–5 minutes until all the ingredients are heated through.

5. Serve with your choice of main dish. It could be Thai-inspired or sweet and sour, but this rice is equally fabulous alongside a simple, plain omelette!

Tip

If rice is cooled too slowly after cooking or is left at room temperature for too long, bacteria can develop that may cause food poisoning. It is vital to cool and refrigerate cooked rice as quickly as possible. Spread it out in a thin layer so it cools more quickly. Once cold, put it in a container, cover and chill in the fridge. Keep cooked rice for no more than a day before reheating it – and only reheat it once.

'Cutting food waste is a delicious way of saving money, helping to feed the world and protect the planet.'

Tristram Stuart

Desserts, Bakes and Treats

Strawberry granita
With basil and balsamic syrup (v)

If you're someone who buys reduced-price strawberries to dodge the high price tag, finding squishy strawberries in your fridge 2 days later needn't be problem. If they don't look appetising served up whole, blitz them into this refreshing dessert instead.

Prep 15 mins / **Freeze** 4 hrs / **Serves** 4

Ingredients

80g caster sugar

80ml water

400g strawberries, stalks removed

Handful of fresh basil leaves

1 tsp lemon juice

For the balsamic syrup

1 tbsp caster sugar

150ml balsamic vinegar

Sprigs of mint, to garnish

Method

1. Put the caster sugar and water in a saucepan and gently heat. Stir occasionally until the sugar has completely dissolved.

2. Put the strawberries, basil and lemon juice in a blender and blend into a purée. Add to the saucepan with the sugar and water. Increase the heat and simmer for 5 minutes, or until slightly thickened. Strain the mixture through a sieve and leave to cool.

3. Pour the cooled mixture into a freezer-friendly container. Freeze for 4 hours, shuffling the mixture with a fork once every hour. When the mixture has turned into ice crystals, it's ready.

4. Whilst the granita is in the freezer, make the balsamic syrup. Put the caster sugar and balsamic vinegar into a small saucepan and stir over a gentle heat until the sugar has completely dissolved. Turn up the heat and leave the liquid to simmer until it has reduced by half. Remove from the heat and leave to cool completely.

5. Serve the granita drizzled with the syrup. Garnish with a sprig of mint.

Dark chocolate crisp

With granola and pumpkin seeds (v)

It can be tempting to simply discard seeds from pumpkins and other squash in the food recycling bin. If you do, you're missing a treat – a sweet, nutty, chocolatey treat in this case! Cleaning the seeds can be a bit fiddly (and slimy) but it's well worth the effort.

Prep 20 mins / **Chill** 20 mins / **Serves** 8

Ingredients

Olive oil, a drizzle

1 tbsp or so pumpkin (or other squash) seeds, cleaned so there are no strings or pulp attached and then patted dry

230g dark chocolate, chopped

85g granola

½ tsp flaky sea salt

Method

1. Preheat the oven to 200°C/180°C fan/ gas mark 6. Line a baking sheet with foil. Spread the pumpkin seeds in a single layer on the baking sheet. Drizzle lightly with olive oil and stir to coat evenly. Roast in the oven for 15 minutes, or until just golden. Remove from the oven and allow to cool.

2. Meanwhile, melt the dark chocolate in a bowl above a pan of simmering water, stirring every 20 seconds until smooth. Line a 20 × 30cm tray with baking parchment and spread the melted chocolate on to the parchment.

3. Scatter the granola, 1 tablespoon of the pumpkin seeds and the sea salt over the chocolate. Refrigerate until set, which should be around 20 minutes.

4. Break into pieces to serve. The chocolate crisp can be kept in the fridge for up to 1 week.

Tip

Save any roasted pumpkin seeds for snacking on. You can season them with whatever takes your fancy: smoked paprika, curry powder, chilli powder ... Pumpkin seeds are rich in antioxidants and are a good source of unsaturated fats. So, happy, healthy snacking (as part of a balanced diet, etc., etc.!).

Banana cookies
With oats and raisins (v)

Sometimes, you just miss that moment when your bananas reach their prime. Brown bananas aren't everyone's cup of tea – but there's no need to let them go to waste. If you've already made 10,000 banana loaves during the Covid-19 lockdowns, do something different and try these mouth-watering cookies. They're perfect for breakfast, but you can enjoy them at any time of the day!

Prep 20 mins / **Bake** 15 mins / **Makes** 12 cookies

Ingredients

2 medium-sized ripe bananas, mashed

240g crunchy peanut butter

130g golden caster sugar

1 tsp vanilla extract

90g rolled oats

60g plain flour

2 tsp ground cinnamon

½ tsp salt

¼ tsp baking soda

160g raisins

Method

1. Preheat the oven to 180°C/160°C fan/gas mark 4.

2. In a bowl, beat together the bananas, peanut butter, golden caster sugar and vanilla extract until combined.

3. In a separate bowl, mix together the oats, flour, ground cinnamon, salt and baking soda. Gradually combine into the wet mixture in the other bowl. Stir in the raisins.

4. Line a large baking tray with baking parchment. Divide the dough into 12 portions on the tray and flatten each to around 1.5cm thickness.

5. Bake for 15 minutes in the oven, or until golden brown. Cool the cookies on the baking tray for 5 minutes and then transfer to a wire rack.

Tip
Still got a bunch of brown bananas left? Turn the page for another delicious way to transform overripe bananas.

Roast banana

With rum and spices (v)

You can't have too many recipes for dealing with overripe bananas! Here, the bananas are roasted with nutmeg and cinnamon, but you can dress them up with a range of toppings.

Prep 10 mins / **Bake** 15 mins / **Serves** 4

Ingredients

4 bananas

Juice of 2 limes

2 tbsp dark rum

½ tsp ground cinnamon (plus ½ tsp to dust)

¼ tsp ground nutmeg

2 tbsp coconut sugar

Mint leaves, to garnish

Method

1. Preheat the oven to 200°C/180°C fan/ gas mark 6.

2. Peel the bananas and slice in half lengthwise. Arrange the banana halves on a baking tray lined with baking parchment.

3. Drizzle the lime juice and rum over the bananas. Sprinkle with the cinnamon, nutmeg and coconut sugar.

4. Roast in the oven for 10-15 minutes.

5. Serve hot with a scoop of ice cream. Garnish with mint leaves and a dusting of cinnamon.

Tip

Cooler temperatures slow down the ripening process. Once bananas are ripe to your liking, store them in the fridge (away from other fruit). It's okay if the skin turns brown or black – it doesn't affect the fruit inside, which should still have a lovely flavour and texture.

Bread pudding
With cinnamon and raisins (v)

Bread pudding is a classic dessert for using up stale bread. Hearty and warming, it's guaranteed to put a smile on everyone's face. If you have lots of bread to use up, double the recipe, make two puddings and freeze one! Simply place in an airtight container and pop in the freezer – it should last for 2 months – and defrost before reheating.

Prep 15 mins / **Bake** 45 mins / **Serves** 6

Ingredients

8 slices of bread

40g butter, melted (plus extra for greasing)

80g raisins

4 eggs, beaten

225ml milk

250ml double cream

220g caster sugar

1 tsp ground cinnamon

1 tsp vanilla extract

Tip

Try adding apples that are past their best to your bread pudding. Simply chop them into small pieces and sprinkle them on with the raisins.

Method

1. Preheat the oven to 180°C/160°C fan/gas mark 4.

2. Break the bread into small pieces and place in a greased 20cm square baking dish. Drizzle the melted butter over the bread. Sprinkle with the raisins.

3. In a bowl, combine the eggs, milk, cream, sugar, ground cinnamon and vanilla extract. Beat until well mixed.

4. Pour the egg mixture over the bread and gently push down with a fork until the bread is covered and soaking up the mixture.

5. Bake in the oven for 45 minutes, or until the top springs back when pressed.

6. Delicious served hot or cold with custard or ice cream.

Squishy fruit crumble

With summer fruits (or whatever fruit you like!) (v)

The joy of this recipe is that you can add whatever fruits you have lying around going squishy! Be seasonal – in summertime, you might add strawberries and nectarines; in autumn, pears and figs. Either way, it's the ideal way to use up fruit that is going past its best.

Prep 30 mins / **Bake** 50 mins / **Serves** 6–8

Ingredients

2 peaches, stoned and chopped

2 plums, stoned and chopped

125g raspberries

125g blueberries

125g apples, peeled, cored and sliced finely

2 tbsp cornflour

2 tbsp caster sugar

Juice of ½ lemon

For the crumble

125g plain flour

75g demerara sugar

75g caster sugar

30g rolled oats

85g unsalted butter, cut into pieces

Method

1. Preheat the oven to 180°C/160°C fan/gas mark 4.

2. In a large bowl, toss all the fruit with the cornflour, caster sugar and lemon juice. Leave to rest for 30 minutes.

3. Meanwhile, make the crumble. In a large mixing bowl, combine the flour, demerara sugar, caster sugar, oats and butter. Use your fingers to rub the butter into the dry ingredients until the mixture turns into a crumble.

4. Place the fruit in an ovenproof dish and top with the crumble mixture.

5. Bake in the oven for 50 minutes, or until the crumble is golden.

6. Serve with custard or ice cream (of course!).

Tip
How about making jam with your squashy fruit? Jam-making doesn't have to be labour-intensive. See the recipe on the next page.

Easy peasy jam
With no sweating over a pan (v)

If you thought that making jam meant stirring a huge pot for hours, think again! It's possible to make one small jar without breaking out into a sweat. Make use of any leftover fruit that's on the turn – strawberries, raspberries, blueberries, kiwis or whatever takes your fancy – to create this easy jam.

Prep 10 mins / **Cook** 30 mins / **Makes** 1 jar (around 250 ml)

Ingredients

235g fruit, washed, chopped, stoned, leaves/stalks removed

150g caster sugar

1 tbsp lemon juice

Method

1. In a large bowl, mash together the fruit and caster sugar.

2. Transfer the fruit mash to a large saucepan with a heavy bottom. Stir in the lemon juice.

3. Over a medium heat, stir the mixture until the sugar has dissolved.

4. Bring to the boil then turn the heat down. Simmer for around 20 minutes until the jam is thick and has turned a darker colour.

5. Transfer the jam to a clean jar and allow to cool. When cooled, add a lid and put in the fridge.

6. The jam can be stored in the fridge for up to 2 weeks. It can also be frozen for 1 month.

Tip

Before you compost a squeezed lemon, grate the zest and simply put it in the freezer for next time a recipe needs it. (Lemon peel is also a fragrant firelighter! Simply bake the peelings in the oven until they darken, and then add them to your fire or barbecue.)

Oaty pancakes
With coffee grounds and cinnamon (v)

If you're using ground coffee at home in your coffee machine, don't throw it away once you've enjoyed your caffeine hit. You might be surprised, but did you know that you can repurpose it in your cooking? These oat pancakes have a delicious coffee zing and can be finished with whatever topping you fancy.

Prep 10 mins / **Cook** 2–4 mins per pancake / **Makes** 4 large pancakes

Ingredients

60g used coffee grounds

400g oatmeal

600ml milk

2 tsp baking soda

3 tsp ground cinnamon

Pinch of salt

2 tbsp vegetable or olive oil

3 large eggs, lightly beaten

Tip

Coffee grounds are also fantastic for your garden. They can improve fertiliser, add nutrients and deter pests. Mix the grounds into the top few centimetres of soil or just sprinkle the grounds on top of the soil. Don't pile the grounds too deeply, though, as they might prevent water getting through.

Method

1. In a large bowl, mix together the coffee grounds, oatmeal, baking soda, eggs, ground cinnamon and salt.

2. Make a well in the middle of the bowl and gradually add the milk, whisking as you go. Keep adding milk until the batter is a pourable consistency but isn't too thin. Whisk thoroughly.

3. Heat 1 tablespoon of the oil in a frying pan over a medium heat. When the oil is hot, add one quarter of the batter mix. Turn the pan to coat the base evenly. Cook on both sides for 1–2 minutes. Repeat with the remaining mixture to make another three pancakes.

4. Delicious served with coconut or banana ice cream, with poached berries (use up the squashy ones that are about to go past their best!) or with fresh fruit. Finish off with a drizzle of chocolate sauce.

'You cannot get through a single day without having an impact on the world around you. What you do makes a difference, and you have to decide what kind of difference you want to make.'

Jane Goodall